Minibeast Pets

Centipedes and Millipedes

by Theresa Greenaway

Photographs by Chris Fairclough

WAYLAND

Minibeast Pets

Ants

Beetles

Caterpillars

Slugs and Snails

Spiders

Tadpoles

Worms

Cover photograph: A forest millipede in the Tsitsikamma Forest National Park, South Africa.

All Wayland books encourage
children to read and help them improve their literacy.

✓ The contents page, page numbers, headings, diagrams and index help locate specific pieces of information.

✓ The glossary reinforces alphabetic knowledge and extends vocabulary.

✓ On page 30 you can find out about other books, videos, CD-ROMs and websites dealing with the same subject.

© Copyright 2000 (text) Wayland Publishers Limited
61 Western Road, Hove, East Sussex BN3 1JD

Planned and produced by Discovery Books Limited
Project Editors: Patience Coster and Pam Wells
Project Manager: Joyce Spicer
Illustrated by Colin Newman and Stefan Chabluk
Designed by Ian Winton

British Library Cataloguing in Publication Data
Greenaway, Theresa
   Centipedes and Millipedes. – (Minibeast Pets)
   1. Centipedes – Juvenile literature
   2. Millipedes – Juvenile literature
   3. Millipedes as pets - Juvenile literature
   I. Title
   595.6'2

HARDBACK   ISBN 0 7502 2687 0
PAPERBACK   ISBN 0 7502 2741 9

Printed and bound in the USA

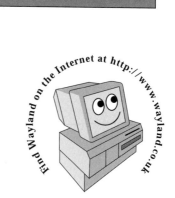

Find Wayland on the Internet at http://www.wayland.co.uk

WARNING
Some centipedes bite. Do not pick them up with your bare hands unless you know they do not bite. Ask an adult to help you identify which types of centipedes can bite.

Contents

What's the difference?

Centipedes and millipedes are invertebrates, or animals without backbones. They both have lots of legs and long bodies made up of a chain of parts, called segments. This makes millipedes and centipedes appear similar at first, but they are really quite different.

Centipedes have one pair of legs on each segment. You may need to use a magnifying glass to see this clearly. Their bodies are flattened and they run around very fast, hiding in even the smallest cracks. They are often yellowish or an orange-brown colour.

Centipedes

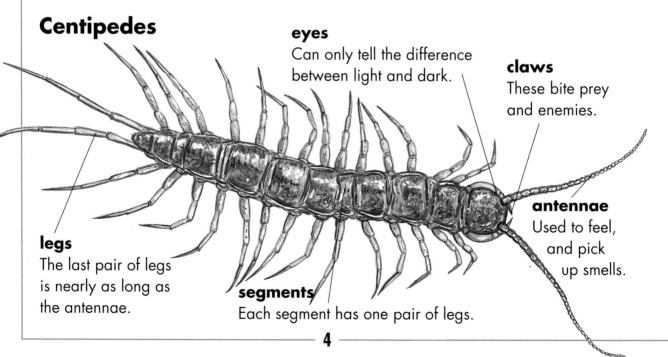

eyes
Can only tell the difference between light and dark.

claws
These bite prey and enemies.

antennae
Used to feel, and pick up smells.

legs
The last pair of legs is nearly as long as the antennae.

segments
Each segment has one pair of legs.

Centipedes are fierce hunters – catching and eating other invertebrates, even other centipedes. The centipede's first pair of legs are sharp, pointed claws that curve forward and look just like fangs. These pinch prey or enemies and inject a painful, poisonous venom.

Millipedes

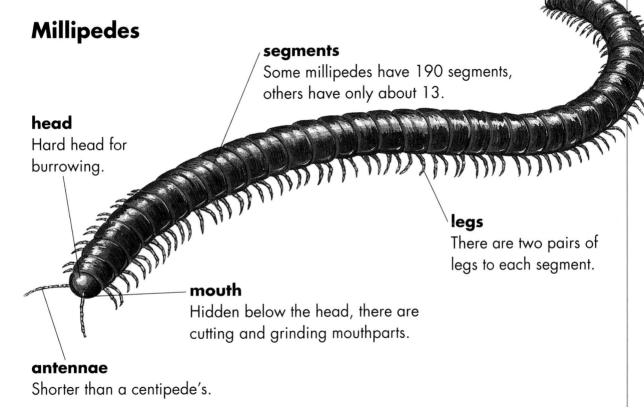

segments
Some millipedes have 190 segments, others have only about 13.

head
Hard head for burrowing.

legs
There are two pairs of legs to each segment.

mouth
Hidden below the head, there are cutting and grinding mouthparts.

antennae
Shorter than a centipede's.

Millipedes have two pairs of legs on each segment. They are often black or dark in colour. Millipedes move around much more slowly than centipedes. You will definitely need to use a magnifying glass to look at a millipede's legs. Millipedes eat rotting wood, dead plants and fallen leaves. They are what biologists call 'detritus-eaters'.

Finding your pets

Centipedes and millipedes can be found all over the world. Most millipedes live in the fallen leaves of the forest floor. But some live on grassy plains, in deserts, and even in caves. Many of the largest types live in the warm Tropics. Some types of South American millipedes can survive underwater when the Amazon region floods.

▼ Millipedes from warm countries are often more brightly coloured than those from cooler countries.

Most types of centipedes also live in warm countries. Some spend their lives underground. Others hide under stones during the day and come out at night to hunt. There are even a few types of centipedes that can live on the seashore.

There are plenty of centipedes and millipedes in gardens and parks, too. Look for them under stones, in rotting logs, or in the compost heap. When gardeners are digging, they come across them in the soil. Centipedes hate the light. As soon as they are uncovered, they run for shelter.

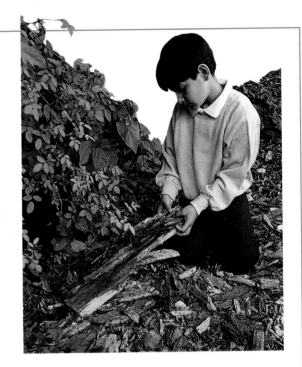

▶ Lifting up pieces of wood or logs is a good way to find centipedes and millipedes.

Lots of legs

'Centi' means a hundred and 'milli' means a thousand. Centipedes may have anything between thirty and over a hundred legs, but millipedes never have as many as their name suggests. This polydesmid millipede has around eighty legs.

Collecting your pets

Collect a trowel, some jars or plastic containers and lids with holes in their lids, a plastic spoon, a small pot, a notebook and pencil. Label or number the jars. Now you are ready to start searching.

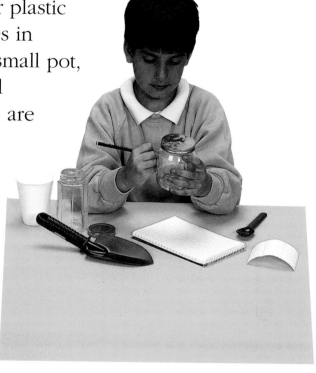

Use your trowel to dig carefully into the soil. The plastic spoon makes picking up millipedes easy. You will need a spoon and a little pot to collect the much faster centipedes.

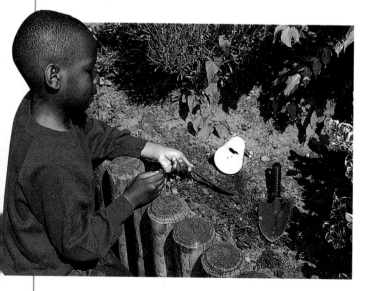

Do not use your fingers to pick up centipedes. Remember that even the small ones can pinch with their fang-like claws. Collect centipedes by guiding them with the spoon into a small container. Then transfer them to labelled jars.

◄ It takes practise to catch your pets!

▲ A centipede hunts for tiny animals among moss and dead leaves.

Place some decaying leaves in the bottom of the jars. Put only one centipede into each jar – or the biggest may eat the others. Write down in your notebook exactly where you found each of your new pets.

Pitfall traps are another good way to catch centipedes and millipedes. Sink a plastic container into the ground. Cover it with a flat stone supported by small pebbles. Check every hour or so to see if anything has fallen into it.

◄ A pitfall trap.

Making a home

To keep centipedes and millipedes alive, you need to make their new home as much like their old one as possible. Since millipedes do not eat each other, several can be kept together in a large container. Put about 3 cm of loose soil at the bottom of the container, then add a thick layer of fallen leaves. Place a piece of rotting wood and a small pile of pebbles on the soil. Plant small tufts of grass.

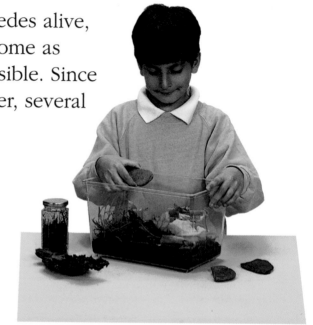

You can make the same type of home for your centipedes, but do not keep too many together at once. The soil needs to be deeper, about 8 cm. Put rotting wood and pebbles, or small rocks, on to the soil.

grass

rotting wood

soil

pebbles

leaves

Keep the soil and leaves of all the homes slightly moist, but not too wet. You will need a lid with small holes in it for each one. Make sure that your pet homes do not stand in direct sunlight all day long.

Backwards and forwards

Garden centipedes hunt in soil or among stones. A centipede has a pair of long antennae (feelers) on its head. These help it to detect prey and enemies. To escape from danger, a centipede sometimes has to run backwards. Its back pair of legs are long and trailing. They work just like feelers.

Feeding your pets

Most types of millipedes eat decaying leaves and other small pieces of dead plants. Some will eat the kind of plant matter found in a compost heap. But they can be quite fussy and prefer some kinds of leaves to others.

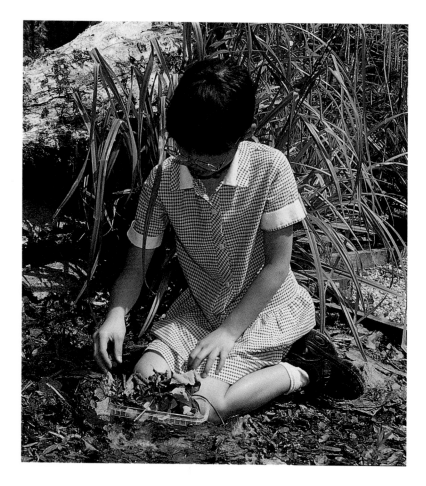

Collect different kinds of dry autumn leaves from the ground under oak, ash, maple, or birch trees. See what your pets like best. If some of your millipedes were collected from a compost heap, try putting an apple peel, an orange peel, or a slice of raw potato into their home. The next morning, carefully look underneath the food to see if any of the millipedes are under it or feeding on it.

▶ This centipede is eating a caterpillar that it has killed by injecting it with venom.

Centipedes are harder to keep well fed, since they need living prey. You should collect tiny worms and small beetles for them to eat.

Have a feeding area of soil or rotting wood that you replace every other day. Your centipedes can hunt through this and feed on the tiny creatures living in it. But be very careful not to throw any centipedes away when you change this soil or wood.

Looking after your pets

Centipedes and millipedes are not too difficult to look after. Remember to check your notes on where you found them. Then, you can keep their new homes as much like their old one as possible.

Do not let their home dry out. Keep some parts quite dry, but other areas damp. A tuft of moss planted in the damper area will give your pets somewhere to hide. Use a fine spray to moisten the areas you want to keep damp. That way, the centipedes and millipedes can choose for themselves where they want to go. Remove old, uneaten food after a day or so, or it will become mouldy.

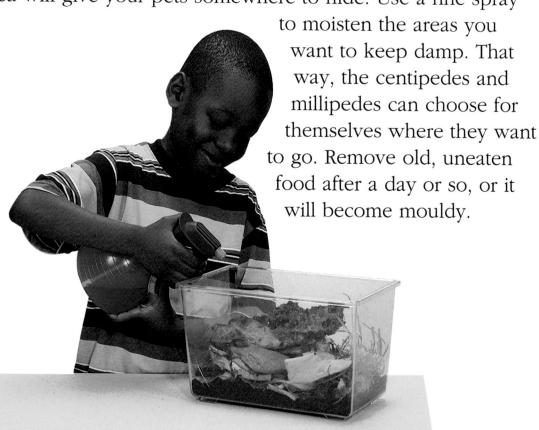

Top speed

With so many legs, it is amazing that a centipede can run so quickly without tripping. But only one leg out of every eight is touching the ground at any one time. In each pair of legs, one is always moving forward as the other moves backward.

Centipedes and millipedes have poor eyesight. They rely on the senses of smell and touch to find their way around. Centipedes detect their prey by feeling the vibrations that the victim makes as it moves around. Centipedes and millipedes use their antennae to pick up smells and to feel their way along. Watch how they use their antennae when they find something new in their home.

Watching your pets

Centipedes and millipedes are shy creatures that do not like bright light. If they ran around on the surface of the ground during the day, they would be eaten by hungry birds. So the best time to watch them is after dark. Shine a small torch into their home. Can you see any of your pets searching for food above ground?

Bulldozing

When a millipede walks, many of its legs touch the ground at the same time. It also has a hard head. This means that the millipede can push through objects like a bulldozer. Its legs give it a lot of 'push', so it can force its way through rotting wood or down into the soil.

Watch how centipedes and millipedes move. To do this, put one of them into a small, shallow container lined with part of a paper towel. Put a clear lid or food wrap over the top, or it may escape.

Use a magnifying glass to get a close-up view of it walking. Look at your pet's jointed body as it twists and turns corners and climbs over stones. A millipede has a much more tube-shaped body than a centipede. Do millipedes and centipedes bend in the same way?

▼ This giant millipede is cleaning its legs. It could take a long time!

Self-defence

In the wild, centipedes and millipedes have ways of avoiding danger and looking after themselves. They can hide by running into narrow cracks or wriggling down into the soil. Some types of millipedes simply coil into a spiral or roll up into a tight ball when disturbed. Keeping very still can be a good way of hiding.

▲ If coiling into a spiral does not work as protection, this South African millipede can make an awful smell!

Some tropical millipedes have an even better way of looking after themselves. They use chemical warfare. When attacked, these large millipedes ooze or squirt vile-smelling chemicals from tiny holes in their cuticle, or outer skin.

These chemicals taste awful as well. To let predators know they have a chemical defence, these millipedes have a warning pattern of black and orange stripes.

Centipedes usually rely on the venom they inject with their large front claws to protect themselves. This poison can paralyse their prey and cause intense pain to small animals. Long-legged garden centipedes can also shed a few legs if they are attacked. These twitch for a while, just long enough to distract the predator, while the centipede quickly escapes.

A bad taste

A red-fronted lemur from Madagascar knows that giant millipedes produce a terrible-tasting slime. But these millipedes make a good meal for a hungry lemur.

To get rid of the slime, the lemur rolls the millipede in its hands and dribbles on it. Then it wipes away the smelly slime, often using its tail as a wiper. After that, it crunches up the millipede in its jaws.

Multiplication

Like other animals, centipedes and millipedes need to get together in pairs in order to mate and lay eggs. If you have more than one of the same kind, the chances are that your minibeast pets may breed.

Some kinds of millipedes make small nests for their eggs by shaping their droppings with saliva. These females may guard their nests. Young millipedes look like short grubs, with only a few pairs of legs. They have to moult several times before they look the same as their parents.

▲ These brightly coloured millipedes from Venezuela are mating.

This centipede, from a tropical rain forest, is looking after her eggs. She has to keep them clean, otherwise they will become mouldy and die.

Many types of female centipedes cover their freshly laid eggs with sticky mucus. A thin layer of soil sticks to the mucus, which makes the eggs very hard for predators to find. Because this disguise is so good, the centipede does not need to look after them. Other types of female centipede guard their eggs and young in a small underground chamber for about eight weeks. Young centipedes also moult several times before they are fully grown adults.

Keeping a record

There are about 2,000 different types of centipedes and about 8,000 different types of millipedes. Of course, you will not be able to find all of these types! Identifying centipedes and millipedes can be a bit difficult. Use a wildlife book about your area and ask an adult to help you.

Try to identify each centipede and millipede you find, and keep careful notes about them in your nature notebook. There is still a lot to learn about the lives of even quite common centipedes and millipedes.

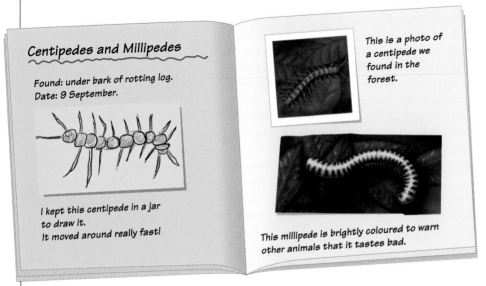

Centipedes and Millipedes

Found: under bark of rotting log.
Date: 9 September.

I kept this centipede in a jar to draw it.
It moved around really fast!

This is a photo of a centipede we found in the forest.

This millipede is brightly coloured to warn other animals that it tastes bad.

You can build up a millipede and centipede scrapbook.

Collect articles and pictures from magazines, and add them to your scrapbook. If you want to find out more, try libraries, CD-ROM encyclopedias, the Internet, or wildlife clubs (see page 30).

Most centipedes and millipedes are less than 2.5 cm long. The largest are 30 cm long! Sometimes pet shops sell giant tropical millipedes. These are easy to keep, and you can compare them with millipedes you find locally. But you are safer watching giant tropical centipedes in zoos. The venom of these large centipedes can be dangerous.

▼ Tiny, pink millipedes from the rain forests of Trinidad feed on soft fungi and very rotten wood.

When the weather changes

In the wild, centipedes and millipedes may move home when the weather changes. They do not like to be too hot, too cold, or too dry. In parts of the world, such as North America and Europe, where summers are warm but winters are cold, centipedes and millipedes stay alive. They tunnel down into the soil to avoid winter frosts and summer droughts. Deep in the earth, the soil stays damp. It does not get too hot or too cold.

Ferocious hunters
Giant centipedes catch and kill lizards, small birds, mice, and toads. The centipede holds its prey in its poisonous claws. Then, it chews the soft body with its mouthparts.

On mild summer nights, when the air is damp, many centipedes and millipedes crawl out of their hiding places in the soil to look for food. Some will climb up tree trunks or walls. If you use a torch, you may have another chance to watch and study these interesting animals.

In deserts, centipedes and large desert millipedes rest in burrows and under rocks during the daytime. They might creep out for a short time at night. But when it rains, desert centipedes and millipedes become much more active.

▼ Curled up in its burrow, this millipede is protected from the burning desert sun.

Letting them go

When you have studied them for a while, you should let your centipedes and millipedes back into the wild. It is important to return them to the place you found them. Check this in your notebook if you cannot remember where you found them.

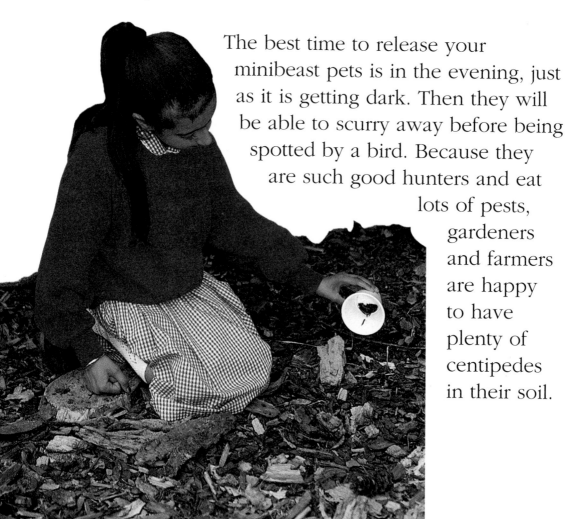

The best time to release your minibeast pets is in the evening, just as it is getting dark. Then they will be able to scurry away before being spotted by a bird. Because they are such good hunters and eat lots of pests, gardeners and farmers are happy to have plenty of centipedes in their soil.

This Indonesian millipede spends most of its time hidden under the bark of rotting logs. If it is uncovered, its bright colours warn predators to keep away.

Most millipedes are harmless to living plants. But a few are not – especially those that like living in heated greenhouses. Do not set your millipedes free near a vegetable garden. They might damage the crops.

If you bought a tropical millipede from a pet shop, do not release it into the wild.

Centipede and millipede facts

Japanese train millipedes sometimes migrate in huge swarms. When the swarms get squashed on railways, they prevent the train wheels from gripping the tracks!

Pill millipedes can roll right up into a ball when threatened. In this position the millipede's head is protected inside a close-fitting suit of armour.

▲ Even hungry ants cannot bite through a pill millipede's armour-plating.

Many large centipedes with powerful venom are brightly coloured to warn other animals that they are dangerous. The tiger centipede has orange and black stripes.

◄ A tiger centipede.

The jumping millipede can make a series of 2.5 cm jumps if anything attacks it. To do this, the millipede draws its body up into a hump and flings itself forward in a kind of somersault. Then, it lands facing in the opposite direction.

Centipedes are not really aggressive. They would much rather run away and hide than fight. But if one is attacked, it will use its venom-injecting claws. Only the larger types can pierce human skin, but when they do the venom causes pain, swelling, and sometimes other symptoms. A baby from the Philippines died when it was bitten by a large centipede.

▲ The head of a giant centipede.

Some types of flat-backed polydesmid millipedes live unharmed among ferocious army ants in tropical Mexico. These ants settle in nests for a few weeks. Then the whole colony moves on, eating anything in its path, except for the millipedes that accompany it. Sometimes these millipedes are carried by army ant workers! The millipedes probably act as rubbish removers, keeping the ant nests clean.

Finding out more

BOOKS

Bug Books: Centipede by Karen Hartley (Heinemann Library, 1999)

Fun with Science: Minibeasts by Rosie Harlow and Gareth Morgan (Kingfisher, 1999)

My Best Book of Creepy Crawlies by Claire Llewellyn (Kingfisher, 1998)

Really Horrible: The Really Hairy Spider and Other Creatures with Lots of Legs by Theresa Greenaway (Dorling Kindersley, 1996)

Spotters Guides: Insects (Usborne, 1999)

WEBSITES

The Bug Club: http://www.ex.ac.uk/bugclub/

The Yuckiest Site on the Internet: http://www.yucky.com

CD-ROMS

Insects: Little Creatures in a Big World (Ransom Publishing, 1997)

VIDEOS

Amazing Animals: Creepy Crawly Animals /Minibeasts (Dorling Kindersley, 1999/1996)

See How They Grow: Minibeasts (Dorling Kindersley, 1999)

FURTHER INFORMATION

Ask your teacher to contact CLEAPPS School Science Service for information on any aspect of keeping minibeasts. Tel: 01895 251496.

Contact the national Wildlife Trust office to find out about joining your local Wildlife Watch Group. Tel: 01636 677711.

SCIENCE
Observing minibeasts
Animal classification / variation
Animal habitats
Life cycles
Life processes
Moving and growing
Food chains / nutrition
Animal adaptations
Animal behaviour
Use of magnifying glass

ENGLISH
Following instructions
Recording observations
Using glossaries
Extending scientific vocabulary
Research skills

ART, DESIGN & TECHNOLOGY
Close observation: drawings of minibeasts
Investigating camouflage / mimicry
Designing and making (scrapbooks, containers for minibeasts)

Minibeast Pets
TOPIC WEB

MATHS
Measuring skills
Collecting and recording data

GEOGRAPHY
The seasons
Weather and climate

PHSE
Caring for living things
Showing respect
Taking responsibility

Glossary

antennae The feelers on the head of a centipede or millipede.

biologist A person whose job is to study animal and plant life.

compost heap A pile of dead plant matter collected by gardeners to spread on plants to help them grow.

cuticle The outer layer of most invertebrate animals.

detritus Fragments of dead plants and animals.

invertebrate An animal, such as a spider, insect, centipede, or millipede, that does not have a backbone.

moult To shed the tough, outer layer of cuticle.

mucus A slimy liquid produced by some female centipedes during egg laying.

paralyse Cause the loss of activity in part, or all, of the body.

predator An animal that hunts another animal for food.

prey An animal hunted by another animal for food.

segments The parts into which the bodies of centipedes and millipedes are divided.

venom Poisonous fluid.

The publishers would like to thank the following for their permission to reproduce photographs:
cover Anthony Bannister/NHPA, 6 Eric and David Hosking/Frank Lane Picture Agency, 7, 9 Ken Preston
Mafham/Premaphotos Wildlife, 11 Harold Taylor/Oxford Scientific Films, 13 B. Borrell/Frank Lane Picture Agency,
15 G. I. Bernard/Oxford Scientific Films, 17, 18 Ken Preston-Mafham/Premaphotos Wildlife, 19 Mark Pidgeon/Oxford
ScientificFilms, 20 Michael Fogden/Oxford Scientific Films, 21 C. B. & D. W. Frith/Bruce Coleman, 23 Ken Preston-
Mafham/Premaphotos Wildlife, 24 Peter Parks/Oxford Scientific Films, 27 Alain Compost/Bruce Coleman,
28 (top) Ken PrestonMafham/Premaphotos Wildlife, (bottom) Eric and David Hosking/Frank Lane Picture Agency,
29 Oxford Scientific Films.